SIX SICK SHEEP

101 TONGUE TWISTERS

COMPILED BY
JOANNA COLE
AND
STEPHANIE CALMENSON

ILLUSTRATED BY
ALAN TIEGREEN

MORROW JUNIOR BOOKS   NEW YORK

Text copyright © 1993 by Joanna Cole and Stephanie Calmenson
"Twist a Twister" by Stephanie Calmenson copyright © 1993. Used by permission of the author.
Illustrations © 1993 by Alan Tiegreen

1 2 3 4 5 6 7 8 9 10

Library of Congress Cataloging-in-Publication Data
Cole, Joanna.
Six sick sheep : 101 tongue twisters / compiled by Joanna Cole and
Stephanie Calmenson ; illustrated by Alan Tiegreen.
p. cm.
Summary: A collection of all kinds of tongue twisters: some only
two or three words long, some that tell a story, and some featuring
a theme.
ISBN 0-688-11139-4.—ISBN 0-688-11140-8 (lib. bdg.).
1. Riddles, Juvenile. 2. Tongue twisters. [1. Tongue twisters.]
I. Calmenson, Stephanie. II. Tiegreen, Alan, ill. III. Title.
PN6371.5.C59 1993
818'.5402—dc20   92-5715 CIP AC

CONTENTS

HOW TONGUE TWISTERS BEGAN
A TONGUE-IN-CHEEK STORY

Once upon a time a king had to give a speech. His tongue got all tangled up. He was trying to say, "Trust train track taxes to triple today." Instead he said, "Trunst train tack trapples to tickle today." The people laughed. So did the king. He forgot the taxes, but everyone remembered the twister. People have been twisting their tongues ever since.

If you believe this story, you're ready for the wild tongue twisters in this book.

Twist a twister,
Twist your tongue-ster.
These are fun
For every youngster!

Youngsters, oldsters,
Join the fun—
Twist some twisters,
Trick your tongue!

GETTING STARTED

Warm up your tongue with these twisters.

Nat's knapsack strap snapped.

Sam's sock shop stocks short spotted socks.

Rubber baby buggy bumpers.

Andy ran to the Andes from the Indies in his undies.

Shirley sewed Sly's shirt shut.

Pick up six pick-up sticks quickly.

SHEEPISH SHAYINGS...
ER, WE MEAN SHEEPISH *SAYINGS*

Six sick sheep.
The sixth sick sheep is the sheik's sixth sheep.

Sheep shouldn't sleep in a shack.
Sheep should sleep in a shed.

Say, does this sheet shop serve sheep, sir?

Sam shaved seven shy sheep.
Seven shaved sheep shivered shyly.

Seasick sheep sail slowly.

NIGHT, NIGHT!

You've no need to light a night-light
On a light night like tonight.
For a night-light's light's a slight light,
And tonight's a night that's light.
When a night's light, like tonight's light,
It is really not quite right
To light night-lights with their slight lights
On a light night like tonight.

"Night, night," said the knight to the knight one night.

Nine nice night nurses nursing nicely.

FAST FOOD

See how fast you can say these tongue twisters about food. Ready, set, go!

Fred's friend Fran flips fine flapjacks fast.

A proper copper coffeepot.

Sue chews string cheese.

Bruce bought bad brown bran bread.

Four famished French fishermen frying flying fish.

OH, SAY CAN YOU SAY?

All these twisters have the *S* sound. See if you can say 'em.

Say this sharply, say this sweetly,
Say this shortly, say this softly.
Say this sixteen times in succession.

Six slim, slick saplings.

She says she shall sew a sheet.

Sure the ship's shipshape, sir.

SHORT TAKES

Say these two-word twisters three times fast.
They may be short, but they're not easy.

Preshrunk shirts.

Lemon liniment.

Truly rural.

Mixed biscuits.

Soldiers' shoulders.

Peggy Babcock.

Greek grapes.

Aluminum linoleum.

STELLA'S SNEAKERS
A Tongue Twister Story

Every word in this story begins with the letter *S*. Try reading it aloud without tripping over your tongue.

Someone sold Stella super striped sneakers. Stella stood. Stella stepped. Stella slipped.

"Shucks!" shrieked Stella. Sam's silver steam shovel scooped Stella skyward.

Star-struck Stella sideswiped Shelly's shiny space station. "Stay, Stella. Sip some sweet soda," said Shelly.

"Sure," said Stella. Stella sipped. Stella stepped. Stella slipped. She slipped south. Sam's steam shovel scooped Stella safely.

Sam soon saw Stella's sign: Sale—Super Slippery Striped Sneakers.

COULD-A, WOULD-A, SHOULD-A

I would if I could.
If I couldn't, how could I?
I couldn't if I couldn't, could I?
If you couldn't, you couldn't, could you?

Little Willie wouldn't whistle on his wooden whistle, would he?

Shelly shouldn't shake saltshakers, should she?

PETER PIPER'S PATTERN

Some tongue twisters follow a familiar pattern. Take a sentence. Turn the sentence into a question. Then make another question, the first part beginning with "If" and the second part beginning with "Where." Here are two examples. Can you make up some others?

Peter Piper picked a peck of pickled peppers.
Did Peter Piper pick a peck of pickled peppers?
If Peter Piper picked a peck of pickled peppers,
Where's the peck of pickled peppers Peter Piper picked?

Billy Button bought a buttered biscuit.
Did Billy Button buy a buttered biscuit?
If Billy Button bought a buttered biscuit,
Where's the buttered biscuit Billy Button bought?

OVER AND OVER AND OVER

These twisters repeat one word many times.
What makes them extra-fun is that the same
word has two meanings.

I have a can opener that can open any can that any can
opener that can open any can can open. If you will give
me a can that any can opener that can open any can can
open, I will open that can that any can opener that can
open any can can open with my can opener that can
open any can that any can opener that can open any can
can open.

I thought a thought.
But the thought I thought
wasn't the thought
I thought I thought.
If the thought I thought
I thought had been
the thought I thought,
I wouldn't have
thought so much.

Of all the felt I ever felt, I never felt
a piece of felt that felt the same
as that felt felt when I first felt felt.

The undertaker undertook to undertake an undertaking. The undertaking that the undertaker undertook to undertake was the hardest undertaking the undertaker ever undertook to undertake.

If one doctor doctors another doctor, does the doctor who doctors the doctor doctor the doctor the way the doctor he is doctoring doctors? Or does he doctor the doctor the way the doctor who doctors doctors?

SALLY AT THE SEASHORE

Sally sells seashells by the seashore.

She sells seashells on the seashell shore.
The seashells she sells are seashore shells,
Of that I'm sure.

She sells seashells by the seashore.
She hopes she will sell all her seashells soon.

If neither he sells seashells
Nor she sells seashells,
Who shall sell seashells?
Shall seashells be sold?

A TONGUE TWISTER GAME

For three or more players.

One player, the leader, reads the first tongue twister. Each of the other players repeats that twister in turn. Then the leader reads the second twister. Each player must say the first *and* second twisters. The game goes on adding one twister at a time. The winner is the one who can say all ten twisters correctly.

One wise whistling wizard.

Two tooting tuba-tuners.

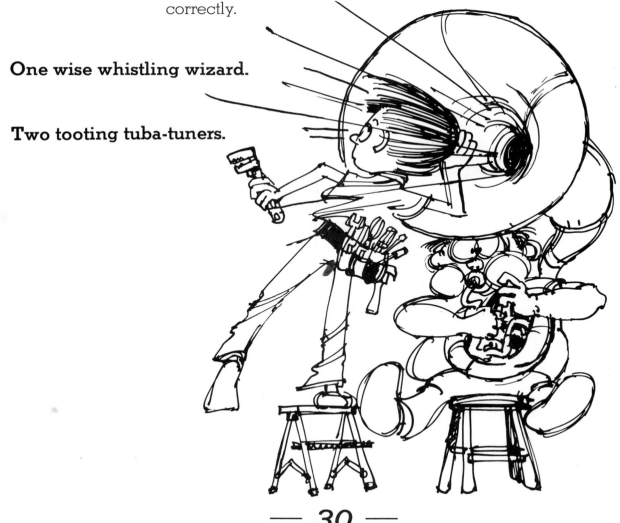

Three twirling tricky tree toads.

Four fresh French flamingos.

Five freezing fleeing foxes.

Six sharp sleepy sharks.

Seven short striped snakes.

Eight eager able eagles.

Nine itching inching inchworms.

Ten tiny timid tigers.

(Try making up your own twisters for this game.)

IMPRESS YOUR FRIENDS

Can you memorize a long tongue twister and recite it without making a mistake? Try some of these.

Mr. Inside went over to see Mr. Outside.
Mr. Inside stood outside and called to Mr. Outside inside.
Mr. Outside answered Mr. Inside from inside
And told Mr. Inside to come inside.
Mr. Inside said, "No," for Mr. Outside to come outside.
Mr. Outside and Mr. Inside argued from inside and outside
About going outside or coming inside.
Finally, Mr. Outside coaxed Mr. Inside to come inside,
Then both Mr. Outside and Mr. Inside went
Outside to the riverside and committed suicide.

Say, did you say or did you not say
What I said you said?
For it is said that you said
That you did not say
What I said you said.
Now, if you say that you did not say
What I said you said,
Then what do you say you did say instead
Of what I said you said?

Betty Botter bought some butter.
"But," she said, "the butter's bitter.
If I put it in my batter,
It will make my batter bitter,
But a bit of better butter,
That would make my batter better."
So she bought a bit of butter
Better than her bitter butter,
And she put it in her batter,
And the batter was not bitter.
So t'was better Betty Botter
Bought a bit of better butter.

Mr. See owned a saw.
And Mr. Soar owned a seesaw.
Now See's saw sawed Soar's seesaw
Before Soar saw See,
Which made Soar sore.
Had Soar seen See's saw
Before See sawed Soar's seesaw,
See's saw would not have sawed
Soar's seesaw.
So See's saw sawed Soar's seesaw,
But it was sad to see Soar so sore
Just because See's saw sawed Soar's seesaw.

TRIPLE TWISTERS

Each of these twisters is made up of three words. Say them fast three times and see how you do.

Three free throws.

Ruth's red roof.

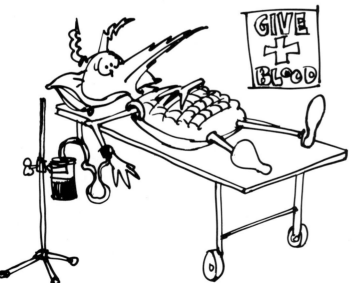

Blue bug's blood.

Please freeze cheese.

Supper at sixish.

Unique New York.

Fred's fruit float.

Plain plum bun.

Miss Matthew's myth.

Sixty sticky thumbs.

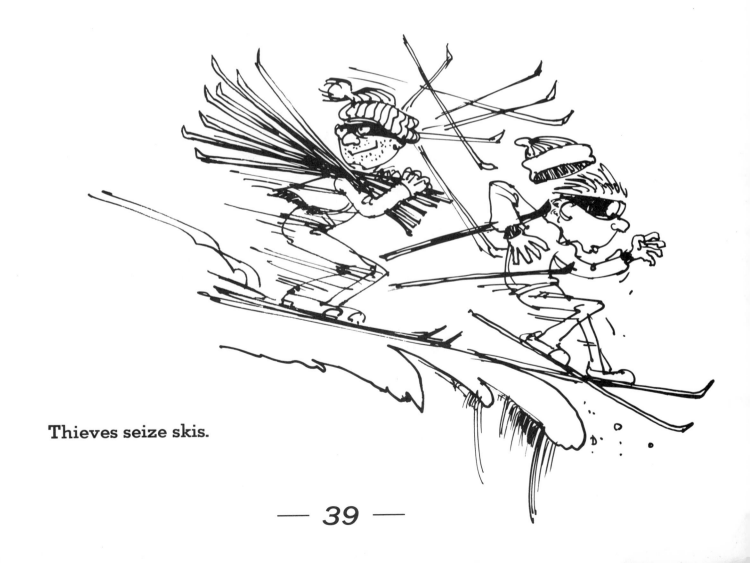

Thieves seize skis.

HE SAW, SHE SAW

I was looking back
To see if she was looking back
To see if I was looking back
To see if she was looking back at me.

I saw Esau kissing Kate,
And Kate saw I saw Esau,
And Esau saw that I saw Kate,
And Kate saw I saw Esau saw.

ANIMALS, ANIMALS

How much wood would a woodchuck chuck
If a woodchuck could chuck wood?
A woodchuck would chuck as much wood
As a woodchuck could chuck
If a woodchuck could chuck wood.

Five fat frogs fly past fast.
The fattest frog passes fastest.

Swan swam over the sea.
Swim, swan, swim!
Swan swam back again.
Well swum, swan!

A skunk sat on a stump.
The stump thunk the skunk stunk.
The skunk thunk the stump stunk.

ALPHABET GAME

You can play this game by yourself, simply making up a twister for each letter of the alphabet. For more players, the first player must make up a tongue twister for the letter *A*. The next player makes up one for *B*, and so on in turn.

Tips for making twisters: Think of sounds that confuse the tongue—such as *th* and *thr*, as in three thin thumbs; *f*, *fr*, and *fl*, as in fat flying frogs; or *s* and *sh*, as in she sells seashells.

A   **Ask after Asta's asthma.**

B   **Bessie bought Beth's beef broth.**

C   **Clowns crown crabs and clams.**

D Ducks, don't drive, dive!

E Ethel's elegant elephant'll elevate Ethel.

...and so on, until *Z*.

T-TWISTERS

A twister of twists
Once twisted a twist,
And the twist that he twisted
Was a three-twisted twist.
Now in twisting this twist,
If a twist should untwist,
That twist that untwisted
Would untwist the twist.

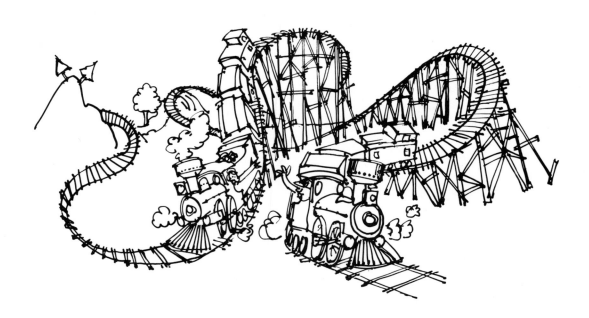

Two twin trains travel twisted tracks.

A tutor who tooted a flute
Tried to tutor two tooters to toot.
Said the two to their tutor,
"Is it harder to toot or
To tutor two tooters to toot?"

SAY-IT-AGAIN GAME

For two or more players.

Each player takes a turn saying a twister over and over again until he or she makes a mistake. The player who repeats the twister the most times is the winner.

You can use any tongue twister in this book, but the ones that follow are especially hard to say more than once.

Which wristwatch is the Swiss wristwatch?

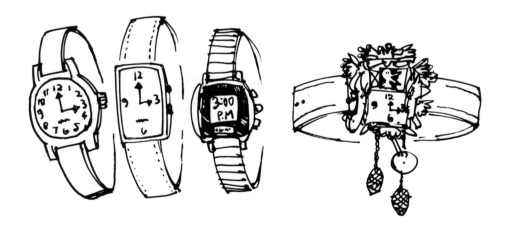

Red leather, yellow leather.

Double bubble gum bubbles double.

TWO TONGUE TWISTER POEMS

They twist *and* they rhyme!

An oyster met an oyster,
And they were oysters two;
Two oysters met two oysters,
And they were oysters, too.
Four oysters met a pint of milk,
And they were oyster stew!

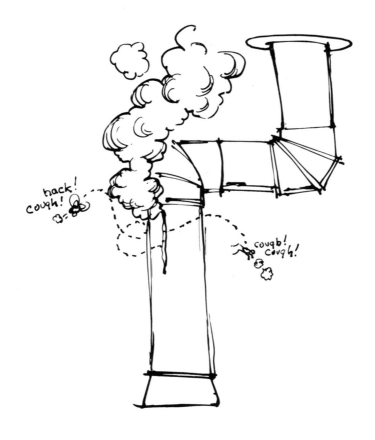

A flea and a fly flew up in a flue.
Said the flea, "Let us fly!"
Said the fly, "Let us flee!"
So they flew through a flaw in the flue.

FISHY TWISTS

I never smelled a smelt that smelled as bad as that smelt smelled.

I often sit and think
And fish and sit
And fish and think
And sit and fish
And think and wish
That I could get a cool drink!

WEATHER REPORT

Flee from fog to fight flu fast.

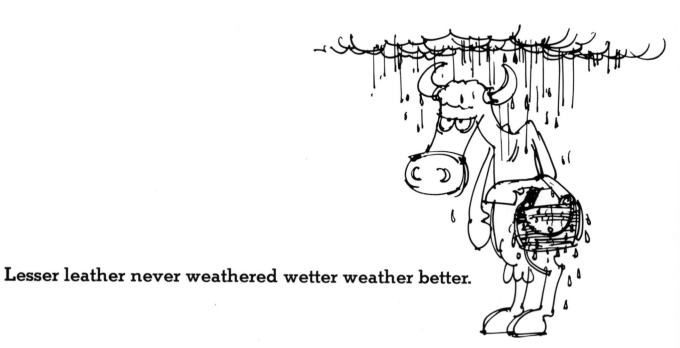

Lesser leather never weathered wetter weather better.

No snow shows like slow snow shows.

We shall surely see the sun shine soon.

OH, BROTHER!

Ben's brother's big black-backed bath brush broke.

A brother to his brother did utter,
"Go, my brother, and shut the shutter."
"The shutter's shut," the brother did utter.
"I cannot shut it any shutter."

OH, SISTER!

Sue's sister switched silk shoes.
Which silk shoes did Sue's sister switch?

This sis sits on thistles.

LAST ONE

Tip-top, tangle tongue,
Say this twister and you're done:
He who last laughs laughs last.

WHERE TO FIND MORE
SOME SOURCES FOR TONGUE TWISTERS

Brandreth, Gyles. *Biggest Tongue Twister Book in the World*. New York: Sterling Publishing Co., 1978.

Emrich, Duncan. *The Nonsense Book*. New York: Four Winds Press, 1970.

Keller, Charles. *Tongue Twisters*. New York: Simon & Schuster, 1978.

Potter, Charles Francis. *Tongue Tanglers*. Cleveland and New York: The World Publishing Co., 1962.

———. *More Tongue Tanglers and a Rigmarole*. Cleveland and New York: The World Publishing Co., 1964.

Rosenbloom, Joseph. *Twist These on Your Tongue*. Nashville and New York: Thomas Nelson, 1978.

———. *World's Toughest Tongue Twisters*. New York: Sterling Publishing Co., 1986.

Schwartz, Alvin. *A Twister of Twists, a Tangler of Tongues*. Philadelphia and New York: J.B. Lippincott Co., 1972.

Seuss, Dr. *Fox in Socks*. New York: Random House, 1965.

———. *Oh Say Can You Say?* New York: Random House, 1979.

Tashjian, Virginia. *Juba This and Juba That*. Boston: Little, Brown & Co., 1969.

INDEX OF KEY PHRASES

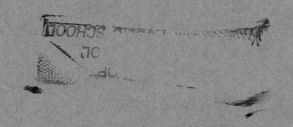